THE NETHERLANDS 2016 HUMAN RIGHTS REPORT

EXECUTIVE SUMMARY

The Kingdom of the Netherlands, a constitutional monarchy, consists of four equal autonomous countries: the Netherlands, Aruba, Curacao, and Sint Maarten. The kingdom retains responsibility for foreign policy, defense, and other "kingdom issues." The country of the Netherlands also includes the Caribbean islands of Bonaire, Saba, and Sint Eustatius, which are designated as special municipalities. The six Caribbean entities collectively are known as the Dutch Caribbean.

The country of the Netherlands has a bicameral parliament. The country's 12 provincial councils elect a first chamber, and the second chamber is elected by popular vote. A prime minister and a cabinet representing the governing political parties exercise executive authority. Aruba, Curacao, and Sint Maarten have unicameral parliamentary systems. Ultimate responsibility for safeguarding fundamental human rights and freedoms in all kingdom territories lies with the combined kingdom governments. Elections for seats in the Netherlands first chamber of parliament, last held in May 2015, were considered free and fair.

Throughout the kingdom civilian authorities maintained effective control over the security forces.

The most significant human rights problem in the country of the Netherlands was societal animosity and discrimination against certain ethnic and religious minority groups, particularly Muslim immigrants from North Africa, Turkey, and the Middle East. Anti-Semitic incidents, including physical attacks, also continued to pose a problem in the country of the Netherlands.

Other human rights problems reported in the kingdom during the year included: substandard prison conditions and interprisoner violence and intimidation in Aruba, Curacao, and Sint Maarten; allegations of police brutality in Aruba and Curacao; lengthy detention of failed asylum seekers pending deportation in the Netherlands; limited allegations of official corruption in Sint Maarten and Curacao; prosecution and conviction of individuals for violating laws prohibiting public speech that incites hatred or discrimination in the Netherlands; domestic violence against women in the Netherlands, Aruba, Curacao, and Sint Maarten; reports that girls from some immigrant communities in the Netherlands were at risk of female genital mutilation/cutting (FGM/C); child abuse in the Netherlands; discrimination against lesbian, gay, bisexual, transgender, and intersex (LGBTI)

persons; and trafficking in persons for sexual exploitation and forced labor in various parts of the kingdom.

Authorities in the kingdom investigated, prosecuted, and punished officials who committed violations, whether in the security forces or elsewhere.

Section 1. Respect for the Integrity of the Person, Including Freedom from:

a. Arbitrary Deprivation of Life and or other Unlawful or Politically Motivated Killings

There were no reports the governments or its agents committed arbitrary or unlawful killings.

b. Disappearance

There were no reports of politically motivated disappearances, abductions, or kidnappings.

c. Torture and Other Cruel, Inhuman, or Degrading Treatment or Punishment

The law prohibits such practices, and there were no reports that government officials employed them during the year in the Netherlands. There were media reports that police and prison staff physically abused detainees and prisoners in the Dutch Caribbean.

Prison and Detention Center Conditions

There were no significant reports regarding prison or detention center conditions that raised human rights concerns in the Netherlands. According to a 2015 report by the Council of Europe's Committee to Prevent Torture (CPT), the most recent independent assessment available, prison conditions in Aruba, Curacao, and Sint Maarten were substandard due to insufficient medical care and material conditions. The report documented beatings of detainees after arrest, delays in accessing legal counsel, and unsanitary conditions of detention in some facilities.

Physical Conditions: Detainees held on terrorism charges at two maximum-security facilities at Vught and Rotterdam in the Netherlands protested the terms of their confinement, including lack of privacy, constant observation, and frequency of full-body searches. In July the press reported on a 32-page manifesto written by terror suspects held at Vught Detention Center detailing their complaints and providing suggestions for improvement.

In March, two prisoners in Curacao filed an abuse complaint against six guards claiming mistreatment, including beatings and use of pepper spray, at the Curacao Correctional Facility (SDKK).

In Sint Maarten overcrowding was a problem due to prison renovations underway.

In the Netherlands occasional deaths in prison and detention centers were investigated in every case. There were no reports of deaths attributable to actions of staff members or other officials. In Aruba, Sint Maarten, and Curacao, there were no reports of deaths in prison.

According to the 2015 CPT report, the most recent assessment available, medical resources at facilities in Aruba, Curacao, and Sint Maarten were limited. In Aruba authorities did not meet the dietary requirements of prisoners, and prisoners with mental health problems and other vulnerable prisoners were accommodated in poor conditions. In Curacao authorities did not provide a full-time psychologist or fully staff the medical department. In Sint Maarten authorities provided only limited dental care, and mental health facilities were lacking.

Administration: Agencies that make up the national preventive mechanism (NPM) in the Netherlands investigated credible allegations of inhuman conditions. The NPM includes the security and justice inspectorate, health care inspectorate, youth care inspectorate, council for the administration for criminal justice, youth protection board, and national ombudsman.

Independent Monitoring: The kingdom governments permitted monitoring by independent nongovernmental observers, such as human rights groups, the media, and the International Committee of the Red Cross, as well as by international bodies such as the CPT, UN Subcommittee on Prevention of Torture, and UN Working Group for People of African Descent.

Improvements: In response to the CPT 2015 report, authorities on Aruba and Curacao opened new police holding cells facilities that met CPT requirements during the year. Renovation and upgrade projects at the SDKK continued.

Aruba started a new prison guard training plan with the University of Central Florida. The CPT and international prison standards were part of the curriculum.

d. Arbitrary Arrest or Detention

The law prohibits arbitrary arrest and detention, and the governments generally observed these prohibitions.

Role of the Police and Security Apparatus

In the Netherlands the Ministry of Security and Justice oversees law enforcement organizations, as do the justice ministries in the Caribbean countries. The military police (Marechaussee) are responsible for border control in the Netherlands. The Border Protection Service (immigration), police, and the Dutch Caribbean Coast Guard share the responsibility for border control in Sint Maarten. In Aruba and Curacao, immigration authorities, police, and the Dutch Caribbean Coast Guard are responsible.

Civilian authorities in the entire kingdom maintained effective control over the regional police forces, and the government had effective mechanisms to investigate and punish abuse and corruption. There were no reports of impunity involving the security forces during the year.

Arrest Procedures and Treatment of Detainees

A prosecutor or senior police officer must order the arrest of any person, other than one apprehended on the spot, for alleged crimes. Arrested persons have the right to be brought, usually within a day, before a judge, and authorities generally respected the right. Authorities informed detainees promptly of charges against them. The kingdom's law also allows persons to be detained on the order of a judge pending investigation. In these cases no charges are filed. There is no bail system.

In the Netherlands, in terrorism-related cases, the examining magistrate may initially order detention for 14 days on the lesser charge of "reasonable suspicion" rather than "serious suspicion" required for other crimes.

In all parts of the kingdom, the law provides suspects the right to consult an attorney. Suspects may consult an attorney of their choosing prior to initial police questioning. Attorneys must be present during police questioning of suspects if a minor is involved or if the alleged offense carries a prison sentence of six years or more. In the Dutch Caribbean, any criminal suspect is entitled to consult his or her lawyer prior to the first interview on the substance of the case; in the case of a minor, the lawyer can be present during interviews but cannot actively interview during questioning. In Sint Maarten, as of March 1, a suspect has the right to have an attorney present during police questioning.

<u>Detainee's Ability to Challenge Lawfulness of Detention before a Court</u>: Detainees are entitled to challenge the grounds of their detention in court. If the decision to detain is overturned, the detainee is released. Compensation may be claimed in the event of unjustified detention.

<u>Protracted Detention of Rejected Asylum Seekers or Stateless Persons</u>: In the Netherlands the national ombudsman, Amnesty International, and other nongovernmental organizations (NGOs) asserted that failed asylum seekers and irregular migrants were regularly subjected to lengthy detention before deportation and noted that lengthy detention occurred even when no clear prospect of actual deportation existed. Government guidelines require that authorities not detain denied asylum seekers longer than three months, but they exceeded this term in several cases.

e. Denial of Fair Public Trial

The law provides for an independent judiciary, and the governments generally respected judicial independence.

Trial Procedures

The law provides for the right to a fair public trial, and an independent judiciary generally enforced this right. Trials take place without undue delay in the presence of the accused. The law requires that authorities fully inform defendants about the proceedings at every stage. Juries are not used. In criminal trials the law provides for prompt access to counsel at public expense for persons with low incomes, the presumption of innocence, and the right to appeal. If required, the court provides interpreters throughout the judicial process free of charge. Defendants may not be compelled to testify or confess guilt and have the right to appeal. The accused is not present when the examining magistrate examines witnesses, but an attorney for the accused has the right to question them. In most instances defendants and their attorneys have access to government-held evidence relevant to their cases and may present witnesses and evidence for the defense. They generally had adequate time and facilities to prepare a defense. In certain cases involving national security, special procedures permit an examining judge to assess the reliability of official intelligence reports without exposing the identities of the officers or releasing confidential intelligence information to the public or the defendant. In such cases the defense has the right to submit written questions to witnesses through the examining judge. The law extends these rights to all citizens.

In Aruba an injured party may join criminal proceedings under certain circumstances. Injured parties who intend to claim compensation from a perpetrator or who generally wish to be informed about the progress of proceedings against a perpetrator should inform authorities in their account of the incident. Police and the public prosecutors have the duty to help victims obtain any assistance or support they require. An interested party may file a complaint with the Court of Justice if he or she believes there has been a failure to prosecute a criminal offense.

Political Prisoners and Detainees

There were no reports of political prisoners or detainees.

Civil Judicial Procedures and Remedies

There is an independent and impartial judiciary in civil matters. Individuals may bring lawsuits for damages related to a possible human rights violation before the regular court system or specific appeal boards. If all domestic means of redress are exhausted, individuals may appeal to the European Court of Human Rights. Citizens of Sint Maarten and Curacao can also seek redress for alleged human rights violations through the ombudsman if the government is accused of wrongdoing. Aruba does not have an ombudsman.

f. Arbitrary or Unlawful Interference with Privacy, Family, Home, or Correspondence

The law prohibits such actions, and there were no reports that the government failed to respect these prohibitions.

Section 2. Respect for Civil Liberties, Including:

a. Freedom of Speech and Press

While the law provides for freedom of speech and press, speech that promotes discrimination and "hate speech" constitutes a criminal offense. The government generally respected these rights in other areas. An independent press, an effective judiciary, and a functioning democratic political system combined to promote freedom of speech and of the press.

<u>Freedom of Speech and Expression</u>: While the governments mostly respected freedom of expression, it is a crime to "verbally or in writing or image deliberately offend a group of people because of their race, their religion or beliefs, their sexual orientation, or their physical, psychological, or mental disability." Statements that targeted a philosophy or religion, as opposed to a group of persons, are not considered criminal hate speech under the statute. The penalties for violating the law against offensive language include imprisonment for a maximum of two years, a fine of up to 8,100 euros ($8,900), or both. In Aruba the penalties for this offense are imprisonment for a maximum of one year or a fine of 10,000 Aruba florins ($5,700). In the Netherlands there are restrictions on the sale of the book *Mein Kampf* and the display of swastika symbols with the intent to refer to Nazism.

During 2015 authorities prosecuted and convicted several persons for speech that promoted discrimination or hatred. On June 13, a court convicted a man for inciting violence against a person because of his race or religion and for insulting a group of persons. The court sentenced him to two weeks of imprisonment. The individual had posted signs in his windows reading, "Turks go away" and "Gas Jews" with a swastika.

During the year authorities held several preliminary court sessions in the case of Freedom Party leader Geert Wilders, who was accused of inciting discrimination and hatred at a 2014 political rally during which he provoked his supporters into chanting in favor of "fewer" Moroccans. Thousands of persons subsequently filed a complaint with police against Wilders on grounds of discrimination. Wilders defended his statement on the grounds of free speech. His trial started on October 31.

<u>Press and Media Freedoms</u>: Independent media in the kingdom were active and expressed a wide variety of views without restriction. The law's restrictions on "hate speech" applied to the print media but only occasionally were enforced. Disputes occasionally arose over journalists' right to protect their sources.

Internet Freedom

The governments did not restrict or disrupt access to the internet or censor online content, and there were no credible reports that the governments monitored private online communications without appropriate legal authority. The internet was widely available in the kingdom and used by citizens. According to the most recent available statistics compiled by the International Telecommunication Union, in 2014 just more than 93 percent of the Netherlands' population used the internet.

Authorities continued to pursue policies to prevent what they considered incitement to discrimination on the internet. They operated a hotline for persons to report discriminatory phrases and hate speech with the principal aim of having them removed. During the year courts convicted a number of persons on these grounds. On June 13, Dutch courts convicted a man of posting offensive and discriminatory anti-Semitic language on his Facebook page. The court sentenced him to three week's imprisonment, which resulted in a two-week suspended sentence and two years of probation.

Academic Freedom and Cultural Events

There were no government restrictions on academic freedom or cultural events.

b. Freedom of Peaceful Assembly and Association

The law provides for the freedom of assembly and association, and the governments generally respected these rights.

c. Freedom of Religion

See the Department of State's *International Religious Freedom Report* at www.state.gov/religiousfreedomreport/.

d. Freedom of Movement, Internally Displaced Persons, Protection of Refugees, and Stateless Persons

The law provides for freedom of internal movement, foreign travel, emigration, and repatriation, and the governments generally respected these rights.

The governments cooperated with the Office of the UN High Commissioner for Refugees (UNHCR) and other humanitarian organizations in providing protection and assistance to refugees, asylum seekers, stateless persons, and other persons of concern.

Protection of Refugees

Access to Asylum: The laws on asylum vary in different parts of the kingdom. In general the Netherlands provides for the granting of asylum or refugee status, and the government has an established system for providing protection to refugees.

Sint Maarten does not recognize asylum seekers. Foreigners requesting asylum were processed as foreigners requesting a humanitarian permit. UNHCR aided authorities in those cases and determined whether the asylum case was justified and whether Sint Maarten needed to provide protection. If so, the asylum seekers received a humanitarian residence permit; if not, authorities deported them to their country of origin or a country where they would be accepted.

Safe Country of Origin/Transit: Authorities in the Netherlands denied asylum to persons who came from so-called safe countries of origin or who had resided for some time in safe countries of transit. They used EU guidelines to define such countries. Applicants had the right to appeal all denials.

Consistent with a 2011 ruling by the European Court of Human Rights, the government processed the applications of third-country applicants arriving from Greece under the asylum procedures of the Netherlands instead of sending them back to Greece. The government stated such applicants would only be returned to Greece once the Greek asylum system meets European human rights standards.

Durable Solutions: In the Netherlands the government accepted up to 500 refugees a year for resettlement through UNHCR. These refugees came mainly from UN refugee camps, and many were Syrians arriving from camps in Lebanon and Jordan. The government also provided financial and in-kind assistance to refugees who sought to return to their home country voluntarily.

Temporary Protection: The Netherlands government also provided temporary protection to individuals who may not qualify as refugees. According to Eurostat data, it provided subsidiary protection to approximately 4,975 persons and humanitarian status to 390 in the first nine months of the year.

Stateless Persons

According to the most recent UNHCR statistics, 1,951 persons in the Netherlands fell under UNHCR's statelessness mandate at the end of 2014. Stateless persons in the Netherlands included Palestinians from Syria, Romani immigrants, and some Malaccans, who declined both Dutch and Indonesian citizenship for historical and political reasons. UNHCR acknowledged that the 2014 statistics on stateless persons in the Netherlands was inaccurate because not every stateless person was properly registered. According to government statistics, there were 2,399 stateless asylum seekers in 2015 and 213 in the first five months of 2016. Most stateless asylum seekers were granted a residency permit.

Citizenship is based primarily on the citizenship of the parents. The laws in all parts of the kingdom provide the opportunity for non-Dutch or stateless persons to gain citizenship.

Section 3. Freedom to Participate in the Political Process

The constitution and laws in the entire kingdom provide citizens the ability to choose their government in free and fair periodic elections held by secret ballot and based on universal and equal suffrage.

Elections and Political Participation

Recent Elections: Observers considered elections for seats in the Netherlands second chamber of parliament to be free and fair, as were the most recent governmental elections in the Caribbean countries.

Participation of Women and Minorities: There were no laws limiting the participation of women and members of minorities in the political process, and women and minorities participated.

Section 4. Corruption and Lack of Transparency in Government

The laws provide criminal penalties for corruption by officials, and the governments generally implemented the laws effectively. There were isolated reports of government corruption during the year.

Corruption: In July a district court in the Netherlands convicted local politician Jos van Rey of corruption, leaking confidential information, and the falsified use of proxy votes. The court sentenced him to 240 hours of community service.

Several investigations of government corruption in the Dutch Caribbean continued at year's end. In Sint Maarten fraud cases against one current member of parliament (MP) and two former MPs were in progress. In Curacao fraud and money laundering cases against two current MPs and one former MP were underway. In addition, a former prime minister was convicted of corruption, money laundering, and forgery in March, but his appeal was pending; under Dutch law his conviction would not take effect until his appeals had been exhausted.

Financial Disclosure: The law does not require income and asset disclosure by officials. For most senior government positions, each ministry has its own regulations governing conflicts of interest.

Public Access to Information: The law provides for public access to government information, and authorities generally implemented it effectively. Persons and organizations seeking information could appeal refusals to the regular courts. Disputes occasionally arose in court over the scope of the governments' right to withhold information in the public interest.

Section 5. Governmental Attitude Regarding International and Nongovernmental Investigation of Alleged Violations of Human Rights

A variety of domestic and international human rights groups generally operated without government restriction, investigating and publishing their findings on human rights cases. Government officials were often cooperative and responsive to their views.

Government Human Rights Bodies: A citizen of the Netherlands may bring any complaint before the national ombudsman, Netherlands Institute for Human Rights (NIHR), Commercial Code Council, or Council of Journalism, depending on circumstances. The NIHR acted as an independent primary contact between the government and domestic and international human rights organizations.

Section 6. Discrimination, Societal Abuses, and Trafficking in Persons

Women

Rape and Domestic Violence: The law in all parts of the kingdom criminalizes rape, including spousal rape, and domestic violence. The penalty is imprisonment not exceeding 12 years, a fine not exceeding 78,000 euros ($85,800), or both. In case of violence against a spouse, the penalty for various forms of abuse can be increased by one-third. In Aruba the penalty is imprisonment not exceeding 12 years or a fine of 100,000 Aruba florins ($57,100). Authorities effectively prosecuted such crimes.

According to a 2011 government-commissioned study (the most recent such study conducted) more than 200,000 persons per year were victims of some sort of domestic violence, including abuse and honor-related violence. The majority of cases involved psychological abuse. In the Netherlands police registered approximately 65,000 reports of domestic violence in 2015. Victims of domestic or sexual violence can apply for financial compensation from a government fund for victims of physical violence. The average prison sentence for a convicted rapist was 20.5 months.

Safe Home, a knowledge hub and reporting center for domestic abuse, was the national platform that worked to prevent domestic violence and support victims. Since 2012 Safe Home has run a national multimedia campaign to raise awareness of domestic violence and to direct survivors to the proper institutions for assistance. The center operated a national 24/7 hotline for persons affected by domestic violence. The government supported the organization Movisie, which assisted domestic and sexual violence survivors, trained police and first-line responders, and maintained a website on preventing domestic violence.

No official statistics were available regarding the incidence of rape, domestic violence, or sexual harassment in Sint Maarten, Aruba, or Curacao. A person convicted of stalking may be sentenced or fined. A judge may impose a restraining order if a person is found guilty of stalking or assault. In Sint Maarten the Safe Haven foundation collaborated with government agencies in cases pertaining to women and children, especially in abuse cases. In Curacao the Victims Assistance Bureau continued a "stop abuse" public information campaign and published articles in its free newspaper, *Tasina*, to raise awareness of domestic violence.

Female Genital Mutilation/Cutting (FGM/C): In the kingdom the law prohibits FGM/C for women and girls; the maximum penalty for FGM/C is 12 years in prison. According to a 2013 government-funded study conducted by the Pharos Center of Expertise on Health for Migrants and Refugees, based on 2012 data, an estimated 40 to 50 girls residing in the Netherlands were at risk of FGM/C annually. Approximately 80 percent of the girls who were at risk came from Egypt, Somalia, Ethiopia/Eritrea, and Kurdish Iraq. The study noted that, for a number of these girls, the risk of FGM/C was real only when they visited their home countries. There were no signals or reports of FGM/C in immigrant communities following the influx of migrants during the year.

Doctors had a protocol on how to assist a victim and how to report threats of FGM/C to Safe Home. Safe Home has the legal obligation to investigate reports of child abuse and could refer cases to law enforcement. The Ministry of Health, Welfare, and Sport continued funding for the Pharos Center to run a project to prevent and counter FGM/C that included conducting research, improving medical procedures for victims, and training professionals on how to deal with the problem. Pharos also operated Focal Point, which functioned as a FGM/C knowledge hub for aid workers, law enforcement agencies, policy advisors, and others.

Other Harmful Traditional Practices: The National Expertise Center for Honor-Related Violence, part of the police force in the Netherlands, received 452 reports of honor-related violence in 2015. A 2014 study by several NGOs and a university concluded that each year hundreds of forced marriages and related marital abuses take place among immigrant communities in the Netherlands. Engaging in forced marriage is illegal under Dutch law. Since March preparing for a forced marriage is also illegal. Honor-related violence is treated as "regular violence" for the purposes of prosecution, and there is no separate offense category or penalty for this type of violence. Laws against violence were enforced effectively in honor-related violence cases, and victims were permitted to enter a specialized shelter.

In 2015 the government began implementing an action program, Self Determination 2015-17, under which authorities were provided one million euros ($1.1 million) annually to counter forced marriage and honor-related violence. Examples of projects included a social media campaign, training community activists, and distribution of legal information.

Sexual Harassment: The law penalizes acts of sexual harassment and was enforced effectively. The law requires employers to protect employees against aggression, violence, and sexual intimidation. Complaints against employers who fail to provide sufficient protection could be submitted to the Netherlands Institute for Human Rights. Victims of sexual assault or rape in the workplace must report the incidents to police as criminal offenses. The Curacao government has a policy against sexual harassment and a procedure to report violations. Sexual harassment is illegal in Sint Maarten. Aruban law states the employer shall ensure the employee is not sexually harassed in the workplace. Employers are required to keep the workplace free from harassment by introducing policies and enforcing them. This includes taking every complaint seriously and initiating an investigation.

<u>Reproductive Rights</u>: The kingdom's governments recognized the right of couples and individuals to decide the number, spacing, and timing of their children; manage their reproductive health; and have access to the information and means to do so, free from discrimination, coercion, or violence.

<u>Discrimination</u>: Under the law women throughout the kingdom have the same legal status and rights as men. The government actively worked to combat discrimination. The law requires equal pay for equal work. There were reports of discrimination in employment.

Children

<u>Birth Registration</u>: Citizenship can be derived from either the mother or the father. Births are registered promptly.

<u>Child Abuse</u>: A 2010 government study (the most recent one available) estimated that 119,000 children were abused annually in the Netherlands. Experts estimated that 50 to 80 children died each year from some form of abuse.

A multidisciplinary task force in the Netherlands acts as a knowledge hub and facilitates interagency cooperation in combatting child abuse and sexual violence. The task force, consisting of field experts, also organizes an annual "Week against Child Abuse" to raise awareness of the problem. The Netherlands' national rapporteur on human trafficking and sexual violence against children independently investigated government efforts and made policy recommendations. The government also continued implementing the action plan, Children Safe 2012-16, part of Safe Home (see above paragraph on domestic violence against women), to improve victim care (including prevention), confront perpetrators, and stop intergenerational violence. The children's ombudsman headed an independent bureau that safeguarded children's rights and called attention to abuse. Physicians are required to report child abuse to authorities.

The website Safe Internetting, a joint initiative of the government of the Netherlands, the business sector, and various social organizations, continued to run a registration center where youth could report inappropriate internet behavior, such as bullying, discrimination, hacking, stalking, webcam abuse, and violations of privacy.

In Aruba the law prohibits child abuse. Penalties for abusing a child could be increased by one-third if the abuser was a parent of the child. The government and

NGOs conducted public information campaigns to focus attention on the problem. Aruba has a child abuse reporting center. In Curacao physicians are not required to report instances of abuse they encounter to authorities, but hospital officials reported indications of child abuse to authorities.

Early and Forced Marriage: The legal minimum age of marriage is 18 in all parts of the kingdom. In the Netherlands and Aruba, there are two exceptions: if the persons concerned are older than 16 and the woman is pregnant or has given birth, or if the Minister of Security and Justice in the Netherlands or the Minister of Justice in Aruba grants a dispensation based on the parties' request. Underage marriages were rare; a 2015 study commissioned by the government concluded that an estimated 250 marriages involving a minor occurred each year in the Netherlands, mostly in immigrant communities. The government began implementing an action program, Self Determination 2015-17, under which authorities allocated one million euros ($1.1 million) annually to counter forced marriage and honor-related violence by raising awareness and providing legal information.

Sexual Exploitation of Children: In the Netherlands and Aruba, the penalty for commercial sexual exploitation of a minor is imprisonment for up to eight years or up to 12 years if the victim is under 16. The country has a national reporting center for sexual exploitation. The penalty in the Netherlands for statutory rape is imprisonment not exceeding 15 years, a fine, or both. In Aruba the penalty for statutory rape is imprisonment not exceeding 12 years or a fine. In Curacao the penalty for an adult who entices minors into meeting for committing lewd acts is a prison sentence of up to nine years. The penalty for statutory rape is 12 to 15 years' imprisonment. The minimum age of consent is 16 in the Netherlands, Curacao, and Aruba and 15 in Sint Maarten. In Sint Maarten the penalty for forcing a minor to engage in prostitution is imprisonment for up to 8 years or up to 12 years if the victim is under 16. Both Aruba and Curacao had two centers for taking reports on the sexual exploitation of children.

Throughout the kingdom the law prohibits production, possession, and distribution of child pornography. In the Netherlands the maximum penalty for these offenses is eight years' imprisonment, while the penalty for accessing child pornography on the internet is four years in prison.

The government of the Netherlands continued to implement the 2015-18 National Program against Child Pornography and Child Sex Tourism. The program was one of the five priorities of the 2015-18 Security Agenda, a national agenda including policy measures and goals to fight crime. The National Police had a team that investigated cases. The Prosecutor's Office and police worked closely in conducting interventions and developing improved digital tools and methods to counter child pornography and child sex tourism with cooperation from the private sector. Law enforcement agencies cooperated internationally in the European Financial Coalition against Child Sexual Abuse Online, the Global Alliance Coalition against Child Sexual Abuse Online, and the Virtual Global Taskforce.

International Child Abductions: The Netherlands is a party to the 1980 Hague Convention on the Civil Aspects of International Child Abduction, but the convention does not apply to Aruba, Sint Maarten, or Curacao. See the Department of State's *Annual Report on International Parental Child Abduction* at travel.state.gov/content/childabduction/english/legal/compliance.html.

Anti-Semitism

The Jewish population in the Netherlands numbered approximately 30,000 persons.

According to the NGO Center for Information and Documentation on Israel (CIDI), the country's main chronicler of anti-Semitism, anti-Semitic incidents, including threats, verbal abuse, and the desecration of monuments and cemeteries, decreased during the year. The most common incidents took place in e-mails, on Twitter, and through other forms of social media.

In April CIDI reported fewer incidents (126) in 2015 (the most recent available figures) than the year before (171) but qualified it as "still higher than normal…in a year without military intervention in Israel." Fewer incidents of street harassment and e-mail harassment occurred. Incidents of vandalism (18) and physical violence (6), however, were considered relatively high. Twice as many incidents (10) of anti-Semitic chanting during soccer matches occurred than during the prior year. Persons who were recognizable as Jewish because of dress or outward appearance, for instance wearing a yarmulke, were targets of direct confrontations.

For example, in a dispute over produce delivery July 24, a supplier expressed his anger by saluting Hitler and knocking down a Jewish customer, subsequently breaking his wrist. The man did not file a police complaint.

In May, CIDI filed complaints with police against soccer fans chanting anti-Semitic remarks.

In 2015 the government-sponsored, editorially independent Registration Center for Discrimination on the Internet (MDI) of the Netherlands also reported a significant decrease in anti-Semitic expression. The center received 142 reports of anti-Semitism on the internet (15 percent of the total discrimination incidents it recorded), compared with 328 reports in 2014. The National Registration Center for Punishable Discrimination on the Internet also recorded fewer incidents, including 46 in 2015 (7 percent of the total number of discrimination incidents recorded).

The MDI noted that anti-Semitic material appeared not only on websites of right-wing extremists but also among the ultra-left and pockets of the Muslim community. The center noted that criticism of Israel's policies and appeals to boycott the country readily turned into anti-Semitism, Holocaust denial, and expressions of wishing Jews dead.

The National Discrimination Expertise Center (LECD) of the Netherlands coordinated the prosecution of cases of discrimination and hate speech, including inciting religious hatred. In 2014, the most recent year for which figures were available, the LECD registered 174 incidents, including 52 anti-Semitic ones. Indictments were issued in 59 percent of all cases, resulting in convictions in 90 percent of the cases. The most common sentences were fines and community service.

Jewish leaders and other political contacts reported an increased, palpable sense of fear among many in the Jewish community and relayed anecdotes of Jews, including schoolchildren, facing harassment and intimidation when wearing religious symbols in public areas in Amsterdam and elsewhere.

The government of the Netherlands updated its national action plan to counter discrimination, which also included specific measures to counter anti-Semitism. In order to counter tension in society over the Israeli-Palestinian conflict, the government fostered cooperation between key figures in the Jewish and Muslim communities, promoted debate among Muslim youth with the goal of advancing diversity and tolerance, and stressed the importance of education to support fundamental values. The government formed agreements with major social media organizations such as Twitter, Facebook, and YouTube to counter discrimination on the Internet. The government also established measures in consultation with stakeholders to counter harassing and anti-Semitic chanting during soccer matches.

Government ministers regularly met with the Jewish community to discuss appropriate measures to counter anti-Semitism. The government worked with youth and other relevant NGOs on several projects, including making anti-Semitism a subject of discussion within the Turkish community, organizing roundtables with teachers on anti-Semitic prejudice and Holocaust denial, holding discussions with social media organizations on countering anti-Semitism among Islamic youth, promoting an interreligious dialogue, and renewing a public information campaign against discrimination and anti-Semitism. The MDI also completed a "counterspeech" campaign on the internet to repudiate online anti-Semitic allegations and Holocaust denial.

The Jewish populations in the Dutch Caribbean were small. There were no official or press reports of anti-Semitic acts.

Trafficking in Persons

See the Department of State's *Trafficking in Persons Report* at www.state.gov/j/tip/rls/tiprpt/.

Persons with Disabilities

Antidiscrimination laws exist throughout the kingdom. In the Netherlands discrimination against persons with physical, sensory, intellectual, and mental disabilities is illegal. The Act on Equal Treatment on Grounds of Disability or Chronic Illness (WGBH) requires equal access to employment, education, air travel and other transportation, housing, and goods and services. The law requires that persons with disabilities have access to public buildings, information, and communications, and it prohibits making a distinction in supplying goods and services. The latter implies that shops, movie theaters, museums, and sports clubs may not refuse persons because of a disability and must provide adequate adaptations. The law also provides equal access to health care and the judicial system. Despite continued progress, public buildings and public transport were not always easily accessible, lacking access ramps. The law provides criminal penalties for discrimination and administrative sanctions for failure to provide access. Government enforcement of rules governing access was inadequate.

In June parliament adopted comprehensive legislation to implement the UN Convention on the Rights of Persons with Disabilities, which made significant adjustments to the WGBH Act.

In the Dutch Caribbean, a wide-ranging law prohibiting discrimination does not specifically mention, but it was applied to persons with physical, sensory, intellectual, and mental disabilities in employment, education, health care, air travel and other transportation, and the provision of other government services. Some public buildings and public transport were not easily accessible in the Dutch Caribbean.

Although discrimination is illegal in Curacao, UN Children's Fund human rights observers asserted that there was a continuing need for more specific laws prohibiting it, since persons with disabilities had to rely on ad hoc measures by government and other employers to access buildings, parking spots, and information.

According to the Ministry of Education in Sint Maarten, children with physical disabilities have access to public primary and secondary schools "if they are able to participate fully in their academic programs." Not all schools were equipped for children with a range of physical disabilities, but the government reported that all children with physical disabilities had access to public and subsidized schools.

National/Racial/Ethnic Minorities

The laws of the kingdom's constituent territories prohibit racial, national, or ethnic discrimination. In the Netherlands members of minority groups, particularly immigrants and Muslims, experienced verbal abuse and intimidation and were at times denied access to public venues such as discotheques. In the Caribbean regions, some instances of discrimination occurred.

In the Netherlands the Muslim community of approximately 900,000 persons faced frequent discrimination, intolerance, and racism, as did members of other minority/immigrant groups, particularly in public venues and with regard to housing and employment. According to the Central Bureau of Statistics, the minority unemployment rate during the year was approximately twice that of the native Dutch workforce, while the unemployment rate among minority youths was almost three times as high as among native Dutch youth.

Various monitoring bodies reported a sharp increase of incidents of discrimination against Muslims in the wake of several terrorist attacks in neighboring countries. For example, the umbrella organization, Islamic Organizations in the Rotterdam Region (SPIOR), registered 174 incidents of discrimination against Muslims in 2015, half of them concerning verbal abuse in the street, often directed at women wearing headscarves; 20 percent concerned discrimination at work or in education and 14 percent involved actual physical violence. SPIOR called the incidents "the tip of the iceberg" because most incidents went unreported, partly because Muslims either lacked trust in the authorities or feared retaliation.

On February 27, Molotov cocktails were thrown at a mosque in Enschede causing a minor fire. Five men were subsequently arrested. They were convicted on October 27 of attempted arson with terrorist intent and sentenced to four years' imprisonment, of which one year was suspended.

According to the Netherlands Institute for Human Rights, discrimination on racial and ethnic grounds occurred in virtually every sphere. For example, many gyms and sports associations required participants to speak only Dutch or prohibited headscarves. Members of minorities were checked more often in public transportation and by police.

The Netherlands Institute for Social Research (SCP) reported the existence of "ethnic discomfort" and "tension among population groups." At the same time, it noted there was growing awareness and visibility of discrimination and exclusion on racial and ethnic grounds. The SCP also reported that up to half of individuals belonging to an ethnic minority stated they had experienced discrimination in a public venue, employment, contacts with official institutions, or education. Muslims often linked the discrimination they experienced to their religion.

Both the government and NGOs, including the Registration Center for Discrimination on the Internet, actively documented instances of discrimination. The National Discrimination Expertise Center, a unit of the prosecutor's department, registered, evaluated, and prosecuted discrimination cases. Most court lawsuits charging defamation involved race. Persons who were not ethnically Dutch also filed civil lawsuits alleging discrimination in the supply of such services as mobile telephones and access to clubs.

Migrant organizations and spokespersons from the black community complained about ethnic profiling by police because it appeared that migrants and persons of color were stopped and searched more often than were native Dutch. An investigation in the immigrant neighborhood of Schilderswijk in The Hague, however, failed to confirm systematic ethnic profiling. National Police Chief Inspector Erik Akerboom also denied the accusations.

Racial discomfort was symbolized in the Netherlands by the continued debate over "Black Pete," the black-faced helper in the popular St. Nicholas tradition. The government officially recognized that persons were offended by the tradition as a symbol of prejudice and racism in society, but it also stated that it was not up to the government to change the tradition.

The government of the Netherlands gave high priority to combating discrimination, racism, and unequal treatment. It augmented its National Action Plan Against Discrimination, adding measures aimed at prevention and awareness raising. The government began a campaign to stop discrimination, stimulate diversity, and deter bullying to ensure safety in schools. The plan also encouraged victims to report discrimination; sought to improve registration, investigation, and prosecution of discrimination; enhanced law enforcement; and supported the use of education to counter discrimination. In addition, police received training on avoiding ethnic or racial profiling.

Acts of Violence, Discrimination, and Other Abuses Based on Sexual Orientation and Gender Identity

In the Netherlands the law prohibits discrimination based on sexual orientation and gender identity, including in such areas as taxes and allowances, pensions, inheritance, and access to health care. The law also prohibits educational institutions operating on a religious or ideological basis from engaging in discrimination on the basis of homosexuality.

There were reports of anti-LGBTI violence. For example, on October 15, unknown individuals severely beat two men on a ferry in Amsterdam because they were gay. The perpetrators managed to get away.

In August the media reported in Curacao a teacher allegedly berated a gay student in front of a class, asserting that being gay at home was acceptable but not while in school. The case was under investigation.

LGBTI persons reportedly experienced more problems at work than their heterosexual peers and feel less safe in public spaces.

The government increased efforts to counter discrimination of transgender individuals. The Transgender Network Netherlands (TNN) worked with authorities and NGOs to advance the rights of transgender persons and to combat discrimination. The TNN specifically promoted an action plan to increase labor participation of transgender persons. Several communities and educational institutions introduced gender-neutral toilets.

In the Netherlands the 2016-20 National Action Plan to Counter Discrimination outlined specific measures to counter discrimination and homophobic violence. Police had "pink in blue" units dedicated to protecting the rights of LGBTI persons. The city of Amsterdam had a safety information call center for LGBTI persons as part of its "pink agenda" aimed at increasing safety and acceptance of homosexuality. When courts find acts of violence against LGBTI persons to be motivated by bias, they can provide higher penalties to perpetrators. The Ministry of Security and Justice started a campaign in the LGBTI-specialized media to encourage victims to report incidents and file complaints to the police.

In the Netherlands the law obliges elementary and secondary schools to address diversity and LGBTI problems. The Expreszo youth website set up a hotline for complaints involving schools that did not comply. The government supported Christian LGBTI groups and Muslim community activists as well as "gay-straight" alliances to counter bullying. The government also continued programs to counter prejudice in immigrant and orthodox religious communities where social acceptance of homosexuality was low. Authorities worked with five gay-straight alliances, consisting of NGOs, unions, sports associations, and other experts, to work with organizations involved with senior citizens, education, sports, employment, and the environment with the aim of helping LGBTI persons feel at ease and accepted. The government initiated the establishment of the alliances but did not fund them.

In Aruba the parliament on September 1 granted same-sex couples the right to register their unions and receive benefits granted to married persons.

Section 7. Worker Rights

a. Freedom of Association and the Right to Collective Bargaining

The laws in all parts of the kingdom provide for public- and private-sector workers to form or join independent unions of their own choosing without prior governmental authorization or excessive requirements. The law in the Netherlands provides for the freedom of association and collective bargaining. The government and employers respected both. Unions may conduct their activities without interference. The law prohibits antiunion discrimination and retaliation against legal strikers. It requires workers fired for union activity to be rehired. The law restricts striking by some public-sector workers if a strike threatens the public welfare or safety. For example, judges prohibited police strikes because of the essential services police perform. Workers must report their intention to strike to their employer at least two days in advance.

Authorities effectively enforced applicable laws related to the right to organize and collective bargaining, and workers exercised them. Resources, inspections, and remediation efforts were adequate. The penalty included fines, and most violations were considered criminal. Penalties were effective in deterring violations. Government, political parties, and employers respected the freedom of association and the right to collectively bargain. Violations were rare.

b. Prohibition of Forced or Compulsory Labor

In the Netherlands the laws prohibit all forms of forced or compulsory labor, and the government enforced them. The penalty for violating the law against forced labor runs from 12 years' imprisonment in routine cases to 18 years' imprisonment in cases where the victim incurs serious physical injury and life imprisonment in cases where the victim dies. These penalties and government resources and inspections to combat forced labor were adequate to deter violations.

Forced or compulsory labor occurred in the kingdom. Victims of coerced labor included women and men, both domestic and foreign, as well as boys and girls (see section 7.c.) forced to work in agriculture, horticulture, catering, domestic servitude and cleaning, the inland shipping sector, and forced criminality (including illegal narcotics trafficking).

In Aruba there were no claims of forced labor abuses. Labor inspectors together with representatives of the Department for Immigration inspected work sites and locations for vulnerable migrants and screen for indications of trafficking based on the Quick Reference Card for Human Trafficking. They found no cases of forced labor or trafficking.

Sint Maarten's government continued to educate business owners about relevant antitrafficking laws. In Sint Maarten and Curacao, front-line responders did not have standard procedures for identifying forced labor victims, which hindered the government's ability to assist such persons.

Also see the Department of State's *Trafficking in Persons Report* at www.state.gov/j/tip/rls/tiprpt/.

c. Prohibition of Child Labor and Minimum Age for Employment

In the Netherlands the government categorizes children into three age groups for purposes of employment: 13 to 14, 15, and 16 to 17. Children in the youngest group are allowed to work only in a few light, nonindustrial jobs and only on nonschool days. The scope of permissible jobs and hours of work increases as children become older, and fewer restrictions apply. The law prohibits persons under age 18 from working overtime, at night, or in hazardous situations. Hazardous work differs per age category. For example, children younger than 18 are not allowed to work with toxic materials, and children under 16 are not allowed to work in factories. Holiday work and employment after school are subject to very strict rules set by law. The government effectively enforced child labor laws. Offenders faced fines, which were sufficient to deter violations. No reports of child labor occurred in the Netherlands.

In Aruba the minimum age for employment is 15. The rules differentiate between children and youngsters. Children are boys and girls under the age of 15, and youngsters are persons between the ages of 15 and 18. Children age 13 or older who have finished elementary school may work if doing so is necessary for learning a trade or profession (apprenticeship), not physically or mentally taxing and not dangerous. The government enforced child labor laws and policies. The government also conducted adequate inspections of possible child labor violations. Penalties ranged from fines to imprisonment, which were adequate to deter violations. No cases of child labor violations were registered in Aruba.

In Curacao the minimum age for employment is 15. The rules differentiate between children and youngsters. Children are those under the age of 15, and youngsters are persons between the ages of 15 and 18. Children age 12 or older who have finished elementary school may work if doing so is necessary for learning a trade or profession (apprenticeship), not physically or mentally taxing, and not dangerous. Inspectors of the Ministry of Education, Sport, and Culture enforced laws and policies to protect children. The government and a tripartite labor commission effectively conducted adequate inspections and enforced the law. The penalty for violations is a maximum four-year prison sentence and/or a fine of 100,000 Netherlands Antillean guilders ($56,000). The penalties were adequate. No registered cases of child labor violations existed in Curacao.

In Sint Maarten the law prohibits children under the age of 14 from working for wages. Special rules apply to schoolchildren who are 16 and 17 years of age. The law prohibits persons under age 18 from working overtime, at night, or in activities dangerous to their physical or mental well-being. The government effectively enforced the law. Penalties ranged from fines to imprisonment and were adequate to deter violations. Child labor did not exist.

d. Discrimination with Respect to Employment or Occupation

In the Netherlands labor laws and regulations prohibit discrimination in employment or occupation based on race, color, sex, religion, political opinion, national origin or citizenship, social origin, disability, sexual orientation and/or gender identity, age, language, HIV-positive status or other communicable diseases.

Two studies published in 2015 concluded that job/internship seekers from ethnic minority backgrounds often experienced discrimination on the labor market. In 2014 the government presented a comprehensive plan of action to address discrimination in the labor market that included tailored policies for specific groups, such as non-Western immigrants, persons with disabilities, LGBTI persons, women, and older persons. The plan contained 42 policy measures for government and employers and employees associations to counter discrimination in the labor market. Implementation of the action plan continued.

Throughout the kingdom the government effectively enforced the laws. Penalties took the form of fines and were adequate to deter violations. Nevertheless, discrimination occurred, especially on the basis of sex.

In the Netherlands male and female unemployment rates in 2015 were 6.5 and 7.3 percent, respectively. The Ministry of Social Affairs and Employment reported that women's higher unemployment rate, as well as their reduced chances for promotion and their generally lower-ranking jobs, resulted from, among other things, their more frequent engagement in part-time employment. According to the most recent estimate from the Central Bureau of Statistics, the average hourly wage of female employees in 2012 was 82 percent that of their male counterparts for similar work. The Central Bureau of Statistics noted that the size of the salary gap was decreasing. Voluntary surveys from employment websites confirmed this trend. The government provided affirmative action programs for women, and collective labor agreements usually included provisions to strengthen the position of women.

In Sint Maarten the unemployment rate in 2013 was 9.9 percent for men and 8.4 percent for women. In Aruba the unemployment rate in 2010 was 10.8 percent for men and 10.4 percent for women.

The NIHR focused on discrimination in the labor market, such as discrimination in the workplace, unequal pay, termination of labor contracts, and preferential treatment of ethnically Dutch employees. The institute also cooperated on several campaigns against discrimination, such as Crossing out Discrimination, launched in September by the Ministry of Interior that focused on raising awareness and encouraging individuals to report incidents of discrimination. Discrimination in employment and occupation occurred with respect to race, religion, and disability. Migrant workers also faced discrimination in employment. The NIHR addressed several discrimination cases; although its rulings are not binding, they were usually followed. Courts occasionally addressed discrimination cases. The law addresses adaptations that employers may be required to make to accommodate employees with disabilities, and the government worked to improve the position of persons with disabilities in the labor market.

The situation was similar in Aruba, Curacao, and Sint Maarten, where labor laws and regulations prohibit discrimination.

e. Acceptable Conditions of Work

In the Netherlands the minimum wage for an adult (23 and older) was 1,537.20 euros ($1,690) a month. The Central Bureau of Statistics set the 2014 monthly income level for "risk of poverty" at 1,020 euros ($1,120) for a single-person household, and at 1,920 euros ($2,100) for a couple with two children. Approximately 10 percent of households fell in this category.

In Aruba the monthly minimum wage in 2015 was 1,677 Aruban florins ($937). In Aruba there is no official poverty level. In Curacao the minimum monthly wage was 1,375 Netherlands Antillean guilders ($772), and the official poverty level was 2,195 guilders ($1,233). During 2015 the official minimum monthly wage in Sint Maarten was increased to 1,553 Netherlands Antillean guilders ($873); no poverty-level income information was available.

In the Netherlands the law does not establish a specific number of hours as constituting a full workweek, but most workweeks were 36, 38, or 40 hours long. The legal maximum workweek is 60 hours. During a four-week period, a worker may only work 55 hours a week on average or, during a 16-week period, an average of 48 hours a week, with some exceptions. Persons who work more than 5.5 hours a day are entitled to a 30-minute rest period. Workers are entitled to four times the number of days worked per week in annual paid leave (i.e., 20 days for most full-time jobs). There are seven government holidays. The interaction between government holidays and paid leave days depends on the collective bargaining agreement in each sector. Collective bargaining agreements or individual contracts, not law, regulate overtime.

In the Netherlands the government set occupational health and safety standards across all sectors. Standards were appropriate for main industries and frequently updated. Workers could remove themselves from situations that endangered health or safety without jeopardy to their employment, and authorities effectively protected employees in this situation. The situation was similar in Aruba, Curacao, and Sint Maarten. In Sint Maarten the government provided guidelines for acceptable conditions of work in both the public and private sectors that covered specific concerns, such as ventilation, lighting, hours, and terms of work. The Ministry of Labor reviewed and updated the guidelines and routinely visited businesses to ensure employers were adhering to them.

The Inspectorate for Social Affairs and Employment effectively enforced the labor laws on conditions of work across all sectors, including the informal economy, with 743 inspectors in 2015. Resources, inspectors, and remediation were adequate. In 2015 labor inspectors imposed an average fine of nearly 9,200 euros ($10,100), which was sufficient to deter violations. Labor exploitation in informal sectors is uncommon; violations were prosecuted under criminal law. An interagency action team identified and shut fraudulent temporary employment agencies, which were known to be facilitators of labor exploitation.

Violations were common in temporary agencies that circumvent labor laws. These agencies mainly hired workers from Eastern Europe, particularly in the construction and transportation sectors, without paying the minimum wage. The law protects workers from exploitation while penalizing fraudulent agencies, individual employers, and recruiters involved in the business. The situation was similar in Aruba, Curacao, and Sint Maarten.